Pacman Frogs as Pets

A Complete Pacman Frog Care Guide

Pacman Frog breeding, where to buy, types, care, temperament, cost, health, handling, diet, and much more included!

By: Lolly Brown

Copyrights and Trademarks

Disclaimer and Legal Notice

Foreword

Pacman frogs are quite unusual in terms of their physical characteristics; they are very unique compared to other frog species – in fact that's how they got their name. These frogs, believe it or not, were named after a popular and beloved arcade game called Pacman because of its round body and large mouth resemblance. They make quite an interesting pet that is perfect for first – time owners.

However, keeping frogs as pets may be viewed as unconventional, frogs in general may not be the best pet for handling. Some people even tend to think that keeping one might be rather difficult. Indeed, for first time owners they could be hard to manage. In this book you'll be easily guided on understanding your Pacman frogs; their behaviors, their characteristics, how you should feed and care for them and a whole lot more.

Embark on a wonderful journey of sharing your life with Pacman Frog. Learn to maximize the great privilege of living with one and be able to share this unique and unforgettable experience just like many frog pet owners that came before you!

Table of Contents

Introduction

    Love 'em or hate 'em, frogs are one of the representatives of the amphibian world! Even Hollywood was inspired to create a cartoon character based of off these creatures. Remember Kermit the Frog? How about that classic fairytale story called The Frog Prince - you know that story where the princess kisses the ugly frog who later turned out to be a handsome prince! Just make sure that you don't buy a frog or care for one in the hopes that one day they'll turn into a prince charming! If you decide to kiss them though, well, you'll certainly get what you ask for – one slimy and disgusting smooch from these charming pets.

Introduction

Frogs and their unique physical characteristic is what make them quite an interesting pet, if you notice, these creatures are often times featured in lots of media – related activities as well as environmental projects. They are somewhat the "face" of endangered animals or amphibians for that matter. The main reason is probably because everyone recognizes and is familiar with a frog.

Frogs in general are also considered as ecological indicators, and the state of their presence is a reflection of the state of the ecosystem itself. In recent years, deforestation and various changes in the environment had an enormous impact in the population of frogs and other animal species. Numerous animals are becoming endangered due to the encroaching loss of habitat, and this warning has been put on high alert among conservation groups all over the world. This is why several conservation and animal rights group are now doing their part to call out the attention of the public when it comes to taking care of such creatures.

Although, Pacman frogs aren't one of the frog species that are highly endangered, it's still important that you as a future frog owner are aware of such circumstances in the environment. If you think you're the kind of person who can take care of these precious creatures that helps in the overall ecosystem – then this book is for you! Read on!

Glossary of Pacman Frog Terms

Advertisement Call – mating call of frogs

Aggressive Call – territorial warning among male frogs; also "territorial call"

Amphibian – Vertebrates that spend part of their lives in water as well as on land. Other amphibians include salamanders and caecilians.

Amplexus – When a male positions himself on top of a female in order to fertilize her eggs

Anura – "tail-less"

Army – a group of frogs

Carnivore – meat-eater, including insectivores

Chorus – a large congregation of calling frogs

Chytridiomycosis – Also sometimes known as BD, a fungus that is deadly to most frogs

Cloaca – Opening in the rear end of a frog which allows for the passage of waste products, eggs, and sperm

Detritus – decayed plant and animal matter that collects at the bottom of a pond or water

Distress Call – call made to discourage predators

Ectothermic – external or environmental means of regulating body temperature

Frog – Any tailless amphibian of the order Anura

Froglet – a young frog that has just finished its metamorphosis from a tadpole

Herpetology – study of reptiles and amphibians

Insectivore – insect eater

Larva – Immature form or life-stage of amphibians

Metamorphosis – Profound change from one life stage to another, e.g., when tadpoles undergo a change and become frogs

Nictitating Membrane – a transparent inner eyelid

Pollywog – tadpoles

Frogspawn – collective term for frog eggs

Tadpole – larval stage of a frog's life cycle

Toe Pads – fleshy, disc-shaped sticky toes of tree frogs

Tympanum – The frog's eardrum

Vernal Pools – Temporary ponds formed with seasonal water such as snow melt or spring rains

Vocal Sac – skin pouches under a frog's chin that are inflated in order to make a call

Chapter One: Pacman Frogs in Focus

Pacman frogs are scientifically known as *Ceratophrys ornat.* They come in many names including Ornate Horned frog, South American Horned frog, Argentine Horned frog, Ornate Pacman frog, and Argentine Wide-Mouthed frog. The name 'Pacman' is obviously what it's popularly known for because its appearance and characteristic is very similar to the videogame game character. Pacman frogs belong to the Neobatrachia family, a new family that is formed under the order Anura species. These species come in a wide array of colors with different markings and combinations. They are generally large and have a very wide mouth.

Pacman frogs may seem like a very easy animal to handle, and although it's suited for beginners, it may not be the right choice for everyone. Before you decide whether or not it might be the right pet for you and your family, you need to learn and invest a significant amount of time in getting to know these creatures especially for first time frog owners; this breed have a specialized husbandry requirements which may be difficult if you haven't had any experience of handling any type of amphibian before.

In this chapter you will receive an introduction to the Pacman frogs breed including some basic facts, different types' info, as well as the brief history of how it came about. These topics, in combination with the practical information about keeping frogs in the next chapters, will help you decide if this is the perfect pet companion for you.

Facts about Pacman Frogs

Pacman frogs are very common in pet trade; these frogs are abundant in the wild, and can easily be purchased from many online breeders or vendors in various pet stores. Pacman frogs make great pets because of its captive – bred availability and low maintenance.

As mentioned earlier, they come in various colors that are all unique because of its special combination of markings. The most common colors for Pacman frogs are red, yellow, green, and dark brown with spots or bright markings on their skin.

In terms of size, female Pacman frogs are way larger than male Pacman species; this is perhaps because of mating reasons. Speaking of mating, males are known to produce croaking sounds while females could not (more on this topic in upcoming chapters). Adult females are usually about 6 - 7 inches or 15 cm while males only measure about 2 - 4 inches or 10 cm (still depends on the breed). The measurements both pertain to its length and wideness because Pacman frogs' body structure is equally wide and long. These frogs can reach its adult size in about 1 – 2 years.

They have a large mouth because they love to eat. They gluttonously feed on various smaller creatures such as mice or rats. According to breeders and amphibian experts, Pacman frogs are always hungry and lazy – they do not move the whole day unless they needed to hunt for food. They are notorious for being lazy and have a huge passion for eating which is perhaps why they have large abdominal structure; they always would want to eat something that is even bigger than them – and if there's no food available at the moment, you can find them just relaxing in dry patches somewhere.

Pacman frogs also sport a row of very sharp teeth – in fact; this is their unique feature because they are the only species of frogs that have teeth! These teeth are used to hold a captured prey. Ironically, this is also the cause of their death because they can't let go of a prey sometimes that it suffocates them. Make sure to not feed something that is way larger than the size of your Pacman frog because it could be fatal.

In terms of behavior and handling, you should be aware that Pacman frogs can bite you especially when they feel threatened. Large Pacman frogs can puncture your hand and draw blood if you stick your finger or hands to them. Like any other amphibian or reptile pets for that matter, they are very sensitive creatures and they also have very delicate skin, which means that you shouldn't touch them unless it is absolutely necessary.

They're not like normal pets such as dogs and cats that you can pet anytime you feel like it. In terms of keeping them, you won't have a problem in making a Pacman frog as a pet because they are not endangered species unlike other breeds of frog. Although you need to also check the rules or laws when it comes to keeping amphibians to make sure that you don't get penalized. The laws vary depending on where you live – check the rules in your town, municipality or state. It's better to have appropriate documents on hand just in case. We will discuss more about licensing later on in this book.

You should also be careful in terms of husbandry because if in case the substrate dries up or if food is scarce, the tendency is that Pacman frogs will encase itself in its thick outer skin so that it could protect them from drying out. They will usually appear dead because they won't move at all. Once they are rehydrated they will shed their outer skin and eat it, make sure that you handle them properly to avoid any accidents.

Captive Pacman frogs can live up to 15 years or more if you properly care of them. Your Pacman frog can be a long – term commitment so make sure that you can handle it financially and also time - wise.

Distribution and Origin

Pacman frogs are endemic which means that they are exclusively found in one place. These creatures are abundant in South America mostly in countries such as Brazil, Argentina and Uruguay. They are tropical species found in these countries, and their habitat is mostly moist forest floors. They are usually land dwellers or terrestrial, their primary weakness is swimming (unlike other frogs), they are mostly found just relaxing in a humid environment or in damp leaves. In the wild, they will eat anything that is within their reach or striking distance. As mentioned earlier, they mostly just wait on the ground and wait for their prey to come in.

Frog breeders today are continuously developing breeding techniques through the use of technology. In recent years, the availability of hybrid frogs became popular; these cross – breeding is also one of the reasons why frogs became quite popular as home pets. All the species can be crossbreed except the Amazon Horned Frog.

Types of Pacman Frogs

Just like other breeds, Pacman frogs also have different types this is because they are found in certain locations in the wilderness which gives these species a set of different characteristics. There are 8 types of Pacman frogs you can choose from, however, some of them may not be available in your area. Nevertheless, it's better for you to also know about them because you'll never know what you're going to get.

In this section, you'll learn about the different breeds of Pacman Frogs, they are as follows:

- Brazilian horned frog

- Colombian horned frog or Venezuelan horned frog

- Surinam horned frog or Amazonian horned frog

- Cranwell's horned frog

- Caatinga horned frog

- Argentine horned frog

- Pacific horned frog

- Ecuadorian horned frog

Brazilian Horned Frog

The Brazilian Horned Frog is scientifically known as *Ceratophrys aurita*. It is sometimes referred to as Wied's Frog. This type of Pacman frog is usually found in the moist lowland forests, freshwater marshes and ponds in Brazil. Their habitat has a subtropical or tropical climate.

Colombian Horned Frog or Venezuelan Horned Frog

This specie was discovered around 1890 in the dry savannas and shrublands of Columbia and Venezuela. They are scientifically known as *Ceratophrys calcarata.* They are also abundant in tropical lowland grassland and freshwater marshes.

Surinam Horned Frog or Amazonian Horned Frog

The Surinam Horned Frog has a large body structure that measures around 8 inches or 20 cm. It can be found in the northern areas of South America. An interesting fact is that the female frogs can lay 1,000 eggs, and they are known to eat other species of their own kind. It is scientifically known as *Ceratophrys cornuta.*

Cranwell's Horned Frog

It is also called as Chacoan Horned Frog and has a scientific name of *Ceratophrys cranwelli.* It is abundant in terrestrial dry lands in Gran Chaco region of Argentina, hence the name. It can also be found in Brazil, Bolivia and Paraguay. These are perhaps the most popular Pacman frog species that are kept as pets.

Caatinga Horned Frog

This frog is endemic in shrublands, savannas, grasslands and freshwater marshes; they are usually found in Brazil. Their scientific name is *Ceratophrys joazeirensis*.

Argentine Horned Frog

The Argentine Horned Frog is also referred to as Argentine Wide – Mouthed Frog or Ornate Pacman Frog. It is also one of the most common types that are abundant in Argentina, Brazil and Uruguay. It usually eats large insects such as lizards and rodents. One of the most kept exotic pets in the frog world. Its scientific name is *Ceratophrys ornata*.

Pacific Horned Frog

This type of Pacman Frog is mostly found in the subtropical or tropical dry forests, sandy shores and shrub lands of Peru and Ecuador. They are scientifically known as *Ceratophrys stolzmanni*.

Ecuadorian Horned Frog

Scientifically known as *Ceratophrys testudo*, this kind of Pacman Frog specie is abundant in tropical forests and freshwater marshes of Ecuador.

Quick Facts

Basic Pacman Frog Information

Scientific Name: Agalychnis callidryas

Kingdom: Animalia

Phylum: Chordata

Class: Amphibia

Order: Anura

Family: Ceratophryidae

Genus: Ceratophrys

Regions of Origin: Argentina, Brazil, Ecuador, Peru, Uruguay, Paraguay

Primary Habitat: Dry subtropical and tropical forests, dry savannahs, freshwater marshes, shrub lands

Adult Male Size: 2 - 4 inches or 10 cm

Adult Female Size: 6 - 7 inches or 15 cm

Feeds On: Mice, Rats, Lizards, Rodents

Description: They are generally large and have a very wide mouth.

Colors and Markings: Comes in various colors that are all unique because of its special combination of markings. The most common colors for Pacman frogs are red, yellow, green, and dark brown with spots or bright markings on their skin.

Primary Behavioral Characteristics: terrestrial, lazy and carnivorous

Health Conditions: Metabolic Bone Disease, Bacterial infection, Toxic Out Syndrome, Fungal Infection, Blindness, Obesity, Impaction, Endoparasites and Water Edema Syndrome.

Lifespan: average of 15 years, but may live longer

Chapter Two: Pacman Frog Requirements

Are you now interested in owning a Pacman Frog? Great choice! However, it is imperative that you see the maintenance costs before acquiring it as a pet as well as the laws involved before actually deciding to buy one.

In this chapter, you will get a whole lot of information on its pros and cons, its average associated costs as well as the laws you need to be aware of so that you will be well on your way to becoming a legitimate Pacman frog pet owner. Ready? Read on!

Legal Requirements

If you are planning to acquire a Pacman frog as your pet, there are certain restrictions and regulations that you need to be aware of. Legal requirements for keeping frog species may vary in different countries, regions, and states. It's highly recommended that you consult first with legal authorities near your area if you can or do a research online or locally.

In this section, we will provide you with an overview of the laws concerning frogs in general.

CITES Laws for Frogs

The Convention on International Trade in Endangered Species (CITES) for wild fauna and flora are the governing body that is responsible in taking care of all animal species especially the endangered ones. Almost all countries in major continents all over the world are a member of CITES including USA, Europe, Latin America, Asia and Australia. It is highly recommended that you have legal or proper documents regarding any animal or species you keep as pets to save you in case of any trouble.

CITES has 3 appendices, and each appendix contains a list of different species in different categories, and therefore has different rules when it comes to keeping, exporting and trading. Due to this you may need to get some documents done to ensure that you are on the legal side of things.

The paperwork doesn't require any approval from wildlife authorities or organizations; you just need to simply provide a document stating the name, identity of the species or your frog as well as the name address, contact details and signature of the previous owner or where you bought it from. You need to also provide your own personal details and signature. This document needs to be kept for future reference by you the new owner until the frog is sold or if it dies.

Certain countries require a special license for frogs or amphibians, and a violation of such special laws can mean heavy fines. In the United States, licenses and permits for keeping pets, exotic or wild animals, and amphibians, are decided on the state level. So whether or not you need a license to keep a Pacman Frog depends on the area where you live, and the prevailing laws in your state, municipality, and town.

Be sure to check not just your state laws, but also your town and even neighborhood laws just in case, before you even do all the legwork of researching the species and looking for where these frogs may be sold, check whether or not there are any legal impediments to your keeping one. If a license or permit is required for keeping, transporting, purchasing, selling, and breeding amphibians such as the Pacman Frogs, then of course you should do your best to comply. Pay attention to any restrictions, limitations or requirements prescribed by your local laws. This includes an almost universal prohibition against releasing captive pets into the wild.

In general, though, be aware that many territories at present prohibit the capture of wild frogs, or the trade or purchase of wild-caught frogs, to keep as pets – as opposed to the purchase, sale, and keeping of captive bred frogs. This is in keeping with minimizing the risks of the spread of the Chytrid Fungus that has already ravaged many amphibian species populations in the world.

How Many Pacman Frogs Should You Keep?

If for some reason you wanted to keep more than one Pacman Frog as a pet, be sure to understand first its nature, characteristics and behavior as well as its husbandry, and the costs it may entail. Generally speaking, Pacman frogs are not communal type of frogs – which means that they don't blend well in a community; they are quite independent and would thrive well on their own. You may want to keep them in separate enclosures if you do decide to purchase one more; this is to prevent competition among the frogs.

Keep in mind that Pacman frogs (especially large ones) are the kind of frog breed that eat their own kind and treat any other creature as a prey. You don't want them to end up killing each other if they're in the same cage.

Pacman Frog and Other Pets

The simplest and most practical answer to this question is to simply keep your Pacman Frog isolated from all your other household pets. This is for your frog's safety and for your other household pets' safety as well. Unlike other animals, frogs, particularly this species are not suited for handling or even interacting with other creatures simply because of the predator – prey relationship that is innate in every animal. The natural exuberance and curiosity of some mammalian pets such as cats or dogs that are used to social interaction will only unduly stress your lazy frog – a creature that is not overly fond of being handled at all and a species that sees everything as prey. Too much stress on your frog is obviously not good, and it may eventually lead to the development of potential health conditions. Aside from that, frogs are also potential carriers of Salmonella which, while it might not adversely affect them, can prove detrimental or even fatal to humans and other mammals.

As to mixing different frog species, again, the smart thing to do would be to isolate each species, but in certain cases, mixing is possible. It is assumed here that you have done your research and none of the frog species you are proposing to mix are known to be aggressive or territorial, and that you are not proposing to mix wild caught frogs with captive-bred. It is further assumed that all of your frogs are in good health and have been duly checked by a professional veterinarian for possible diseases or bacteria they may be carrying. Please remember that the current epidemic of Chytrid Fungus infecting frog populations all over the world is one of the strongest arguments against mixing different frog populations together.

Presuming that none of the considerations above apply in your case, the main considerations you are facing now in mixing different frog species is a question of the size and suitability of habitat. Cramming frogs into a tiny enclosure does not make for healthy living conditions, since each species will need their own space. In addition, frogs hailing from different regions will necessarily require different types of habitat – from substrate, temperature, humidity, water levels, and equipment requirements. If these are not compatible, then do not mix your frogs.

One other concern that most keepers express in arguing against mixing frog species together is the possibility of unexpected cross-breeding or hybrid frog mixes. Hybridization is frowned upon within the frog-keeping community because it lowers the predictability of the type of care that the hybrid frog requires.

It is possible to mix different frog species together in the same habitat, but this is generally only done by keepers and hobbyists with years of experience, thorough knowledge of the frogs they are keeping, and enough money for the needed large enclosure. If you are not sure about the suitability of the various factors that come into play when mixing two different species together, then it is best to stay safe and simply keep different species in different tanks.

Ease and Cost of Care

Even if these creatures are small and seems manageable, owning and maintaining one still doesn't come cheap! The fact is that, these frogs require maintenance which means that you have to provide supplies and be able to cover the expenses in order for you to maintain a healthy lifestyle and environment for your pet.

These things will definitely add up to your daily budget, and the cost will vary depending on where you purchase it; the brand of the materials, the nutrients included in its food and the time being. If you want to seriously own a Pacman frog as a pet you should be able to cover the necessary costs it entails.

In this section you will receive an overview of the expenses associated with purchasing and keeping a Pacman frog such as its cage, food, tank setup and veterinary care. You will receive an overview of these costs as well as an estimate for each in the following pages of this section.

Overall Costs

The overall costs for keeping a Pacman frog include those costs that you must cover before you can bring your frog home. Some of the costs you will need to cover include the enclosure or cage, food and water equipment, supplies and cage décor or accessories, breeding materials, medical care - not to mention the cost of the Pacman frog itself. It is highly recommended that you buy from online stores or websites, legit breeders as well as during any amphibian conventions. You will find an overview of each of these costs as well as an estimate for each below:

Purchase Price: $20 - $40

The cost to purchase a Pacman frog can vary greatly depending on the breed, its age, color and availability. You can probably find a backyard breeder that offers a very inexpensive price, but you cannot be sure of the breeding quality for these frogs. Generally speaking, pet-quality Pacman frog sells for $20 - $40. Buying from legit breeders during an amphibian convention may neither be cheap or expensive. Albino colored Pacman frogs could cost you about $50 - $55.

Enclosure and Screen Lid: $20

When you purchase a frog, you need to make sure that its vivarium or terrarium are somewhat similar to its natural habitat in the wild, so that it won't have trouble adjusting to its new environment. Providing adequate shelter will make them feel at ease and comfortable as a house pet. They may need to get used to you or other people checking them out while they are inside their enclosure so make sure that the kind of cage you will buy will protect them from any dangerous threats around the house including your house pets.

UVB Lighting and Gauges: $50 and up

Adequate lighting will provide appropriate heat temperature inside your frog's terrarium or cage enclosure. You need to purchase things like a UVB bulb, heat bulb and light fixtures as well. Gauges are also helpful to easily control temperatures and the cage's humidity levels.

Food, Water Dish, Tank Heater: approx. $30

Aside from buying food like crickets, mice or other creatures, you may need to provide a watering system and buy a tank heater which includes a thermometer, and hydrometer to regulate humidity and temperature. Crickets is around $2 per dozen, a water dish could cost you $7 and the tank heater including other similar equipment is about $20.

Veterinarian Consultations: $100 or more

Like humans, or any other pets, these amphibians do get sick; you just never know what kind of disease they could be carrying that can also affect those around them. Be sure to save up for its medical needs and vet costs. You may also need to do some medical checkups and/or lab tests once in a while for your pet.

Supplies/Accessories: average of $10

In addition to purchasing your Pacman frog's enclosure and installing fixtures, you should also purchase cage decors such as branches, leaves, live plants and other accessories to ensure that they'll live in a familiar habitat. The cost for these items will vary depending on the quality and also quantity, so you should budget about $10 or more for these extra costs.

Expenses Overview

Needs	Costs
Purchase Price	$20 - $40 (£15.92 - £31.84)
Enclosure and Screen Lid	$20 (£15.92)
UVB Lighting and Gauges	$50 (£39.80)
Food, Water Dish, Tank Heater	$30 (£23.88)
Vet Consultations	$100 (£79.60)

Supplies/Accessories	$10
	(£7.96)
Total	$230 to $250
	(£183.08 – £199)

*Costs may vary depending on location
**Costs may change based on the currency exchange

Pros and Cons of Keeping Pacman Frogs as Pets

Before you bring a Pacman frog home you should take the time to learn the pros and cons of the breed. Every frog breed is different so you need to think about the details to determine whether a Pacman frog is actually the right pet for you.

In this section you will find a list of pros and cons for Pacman frog species:

Pros for the Pacman Frog

- **Low Maintenance and Inexpensive:** Once the tank is set-up, you're good to go! Well not exactly, but you don't need to constantly check on them, they don't require lots of specialized care compare to other frog species. It could be hard at first but it will get easier as you go along.

- **Behavior:** Since these species have a reputation for being lazy compared to other frog breed that put on a "show," they don't require lots of attention and even hates socialization. They can be compared to a kind of painting that you can check out and appreciate once in a while because of its vivid appearance and unique characteristic but it you don't have to spend too much time observing them.

- **Gentle and Placid:** As long as you don't stick your hand or finger on their mouths, they're pretty much a laid back kind of pet. They're not aggressive, dangerous or poisonous.

- **Educational:** Since frogs aren't always the go-to creatures as household pets, it'll be very interesting especially for families with kids to witness and learn the frogs' way of life. It may be quite gruesome especially during feeding time, but it can also be an educational experience especially if you have the opportunity of starting out with a tadpole; you can see its metamorphosis and transformation from egg or tadpole to an adult frog.

Cons for the Pacman Frog

- **Initial Investment:** Even if these frogs are low maintenance and quite inexpensive, you may still need to invest a certain amount of money and effort especially during set – up, most especially if this is your first time in handling a frog. You may also need to keep its enclosure clean at least every week to prevent spread of diseases that could affect your frog, which could also be an added chore.

- **Handling:** As mentioned a few too many times in earlier chapters and sections, frogs in general **are** not the kinds of pet that can and should be handled too often. Its skin is quite sensitive and delicate; they may potentially be a carrier of a certain disease especially if they're caught in the wild which could threaten your well - being. If what you are looking for is an interactive pet, a frog, especially the Pacman specie may not be the right pet for you.

- **Interaction:** They are pretty boring pets or companions for that matter particularly for the Pacman breed. They will just sit there all day until its time for you to feed them, they're not like other frogs that interact or move constantly. Pacman frogs are pretty laid back and still, it's like you bought a figurine.

- **Diet:** You may need to spend quite an amount for their food, and may also need to take note of their eating frequency. As mentioned earlier, these creatures' loves to eat and often times the very main act of eating can kill them due to suffocation.

Chapter Three: Purchasing Your Pacman Frog

Now that you are already aware and have prior knowledge about the legal aspects of owning and maintaining a Pacman frog as well as its pros and cons, the next step is purchasing one through a legitimate breeder or during amphibian conventions.

In this chapter you will find valuable information about where to find a Pacman frog breeder, how to quarantine them, and how to differentiate a healthy Pacman frog from an unhealthy one.

Where to Purchase a Pacman Frog

It is best that you only purchase a captive bred frog. It may cost you a little extra dollars but it is worth it because you will be assured that your pet is healthy and doesn't have any illnesses or transmitted diseases. Aside from that it will also benefit captive breeding programs, and will help them to further breed healthy frogs in the future.

If you choose to buy from a backyard breeder, you may not be certain about its health. You may risk from the issues of importation damages – these are animals that are illegally imported from the wild every year and are usually in poor health condition. These wild frogs may also have difficulty in adjusting to a captive life. It is also not recommended that you buy from local pet stores because most of it is only selling frogs for profit and most often than not some of these creatures are in poor condition because they are living in an unhealthy environment. Before purchasing you should also first identify if the Pacman frog is a captive breed or caught in the wild.

So where should you buy a Pacman frog? Aside from local pet stores, legitimate breeders, and amphibian conventions, you can also get referrals on where you can purchase a healthy Pacman frog from several forums online or online communities. These communities usually have contacts, has history information regarding responsible breeding, and you can also get ideas on how to properly care for your new pet frog.

Quarantine

Amphibians and frogs in general are quite known to carry diseases that may not be harmful to them, but could adversely affect you or your other pets. This is why it is recommended that you quarantine your frog for a few days. It is optional but it is not required especially if you aren't sure where your frog came from.

Quarantining your Pacman frog should be done in order for you to assess the health of your pet and to make sure that it is not a carrier of transmittable diseases to prevent it from being transferred to you, your other pets or your family.

The main reason for this specifically for Pacman frogs is that these creatures are fond of eating anything they can sink their teeth into, and if they are caught in the wild, chances are, they had eaten a prey that could also be a carrier. Aside from that, environmental stresses of shipping, traveling or being in a new habitat can trigger a hidden ailment. If you do not quarantine a pet, it can expose your other pets to potentially infectious or viral diseases.

Here are some steps you need to take for a successful quarantine period for your Pacman frog:

- Put your new Pacman frog in a separate room, away from your other pets or frog's for at least 45 days.

- Make sure to feed and handle all your other pets before introducing or placing the newly quarantine frog with them to avoid contamination.

- Make sure to use separate equipment for the quarantine Pacman frog, and always wash your hands after handling them.

- Cage hygiene should always be done to prevent the spread of germs or parasites. Constantly cleaning and furnishing will help avoid potential problems.

- It is highly recommended that you test your new pet's fecal sample at your vet for diagnosis and testing.

How to Choose a Reputable Pacman Frog Breeder

To make sure that you get a well-bred, healthy and robust Pacman frog, your best bet is to look around for a legitimate breeder. Feel free to ask around at the various frog or amphibian forums online and you may also be able to get a personal recommendation from friends or your local veterinarian. Once you have your list of breeders on hand you can go through them one-by-one to narrow down your options.

Here are the following guidelines for you to be able to choose a reputable Pacman frog breeder:

Do a Background Check on the Breeder

Visit the website for each breeder on your list (if they have one) and look for key information about the breeder's history and experience.

- Check for licenses or document registrations to ensure the legitimacy of the breeder, if applicable.

- If the website doesn't provide any information about the facilities or the breeder you are best just moving on.

Interview the Breeders

Now that you have narrowed down some breeders, contact the remaining breeders on your list by phone

- Ask the breeder questions about his experience with breeding frogs in general and about the specific Pacman frog breed you are looking for.

- Ask for information about the breeding stock including registration and health information (if they have any).

- Expect a reputable breeder to ask you questions about yourself as well – a responsible breeder wants to make sure that his frogs go to good homes.

Do an Onsite Inspection

Schedule an appointment to visit the facilities for the remaining breeders on your list after you've weeded a few of them out.

- Ask for a tour of the facilities, including the place where the frog collections are kept.

- If the surroundings look unorganized or unclean, do not purchase from the breeder or from the local pet store.

- Make sure the collections are in good condition and that the Pacman frogs are all healthy - looking and active.

Characteristics of a Reputable Breeder

By this time you should have narrowed down the best of the best breeders on your list, before making a decision consider every factor to make the most out of it. Make sure the breeder provides some kind of health guarantee and ask about any medical information on the Pacman frogs may already have. Below are some characteristics you should look out for when selecting a reputable breeder.

- The breeder should be willing to educate or explain and answer all your questions expertly.

- The breeder should allow on - site visits, however if you are far from the place, you should be able to request photos or videos from the breeder and he/she should gladly show them to you so that you won't waste your time.

- The breeder should offer a contract and some sort of warranty.

- The breeder should be willing to take back or rehome the frog regardless of the situation.

- The breeder should allow you to reach him/her before and after purchasing the Pacman frog.

- The breeder should be able to provide health records and also have contacts with veterinarian as well as firsthand information about the Pacman frog's overall health.

- The breeder should also explain to you the risks or the cons of keeping one as a pet not just its advantages.

- The breeder should be transparent and honest about how they raised and bred frogs so that you'll know that they're reputable and a caring owner as well.

List of Breeders and Rescue Websites

There are so many Pacman frogs to choose from, that's why you need to do some research and decide which breed you want before you start shopping around. When you are ready to buy a Pacman frog, you then need to start thinking about where you are going to get it. You may be able to find a Pacman frog at some local breeders near your area, but think carefully before you buy whether that is really the best option. Follow the quick guidelines mentioned earlier to ensure the quality of its breeding. If you want a tadpole, you can probably find some at rescue websites, you may also to purchase from the experts at amphibian convention events, who knows it might be the better option for you.

Here is the list of breeders and websites that sell Pacman frogs:

Breeders and Rescue Websites

Back Water Reptiles
<http://www.backwaterreptiles.com/frogs/pacman-frog-for-sale.html>

Snakes at Sunset
<http://snakesatsunset.com/pac-man-frogs-for-sale/>

Big Apple Herp
<http://www.bigappleherp.com/Green-Pacman-Frogs-Captive-Bred-Babies>

Mikes Phat Frogs
<http://mikesphatfrogs.weebly.com/price-list.html>

Kingsnake.com
<http://market.kingsnake.com/index.php?cat=124>

Reptmart.com
<http://www.reptmart.com/p-675-pacman-frog-for-sale.aspx>

Reptile City

<http://www.reptilecity.com/Merchant2/merchant.mvc?Screen=PROD&Product_Code=AP>

Frog Forum

<http://www.frogforum.net/showthread.php?t=10089>

Preloved UK

<http://www.preloved.co.uk/classifieds/all/uk/pacman+frog>

ReptilesNCritters

<http://www.reptilesncritters.com/frogs.php>

Pet Solutions

<https://www.petsolutions.com/C/Live-Frogs/I/Ornate-Horned-Frog.aspx>

Pet Smart

<http://www.petsmart.com/live-pet/live-reptiles/pacman-frog-4033179.html>

Tips for Selecting a Healthy Pacman Frog

After you have narrowed down your list of options to just two or three Pacman frog breeders, your next step is to actually pick out the frog you want. You have already determined that the remaining breeders on your list are responsible, but now you need to make sure that the Pacman frog they have available are healthy and ready to go home with you.

You will probably not be able to pick up the frogs to examine them prior to picking one out for yourself, and doing so is not really recommended. The Pacman frog is not supposed to be handled too much, and manually picking them up in order to inspect them can only ensure that you are bringing home a stressed-out frog.

It remains, therefore, for you to make your choice based only on your observations – how it looks, and how it behaves. This may not always be so easy since Pacman frogs are basically THE laziest frog species out there - moving only when a potential prey is within their reach. Health-wise, however, there are a few warning signs that you may want to watch out for:

- **Unusual Body Structure:** Pacman frogs in general have large abdomens and wide mouth, they're quite large and bulky in appearance, so if you think that the size or body structure of a Pacman frog is not suitable for its age or breed type, it can be a sign of poor nutrition, poor digestion, internal infections, bacterial edema, or even vitamin toxicity.

- **Behaviors:** By now you are aware that Pacman frogs are pretty still in any given day, and they love to chomp any prey that comes their way. So if you notice that for some reason the frog is unusually active, or lacks appetite, be warned because it may not be a Pacman frog breed or the frog may be ill.

- **Skin Texture and Coloring:** Make sure that you study and become familiar with the appearance of a Pacman frog breed. Watch out for any discolorations, skin patches, or redness on their skin because it could be a sign of skin problems.

- **Eyes:** Watch out for cloudy eyes or any sign of eye discharge because it could be an indicator that the frog is ill or had some serious trauma or stress from its habitat.

Chapter Four: Habitat Requirements for Your Pacman Frog

The Pacman frog makes a great pet mainly because of its very docile personality, although frogs in general can easily adjust and adapt to a new living condition, it may still be quite challenging especially for frogs caught in the wild. You may want to make your new pet as comfortable as it can be so that it can get used to its new home, and to also avoid being stressed out. In this chapter you will learn the basics about your Pacman frog's habitat requirements including how to set up its cage, useful accessories, and some things to avoid when it comes to setting up its enclosure or terrarium.

Habitat Requirements for Pacman Frogs

Unlike other pets, Pacman frogs don't need too much space to roam around with – and because it's not fond of "roaming around" in the first place, they're lazy remember? It's one of the major advantages of having this creature as a pet because they are low maintenance in terms of its habitat requirements compared to larger animals or common pets such as dogs or cats. But aside from space, the main thing your Pacman frogs need in terms of its habitat is lots of love and affection from his human companions and of course an adequate living condition.

Pacman frogs may not be the kind of breed that bonds closely with family, largely because of their natural "unsociable" characteristic but just like any other pets you should make an effort to spend some quality time with your pet frog each and every day. If your frog doesn't get enough attention it could also somehow affect its health. And even if they're not as active as other frog species, they might still yearn for attention every now and then.

In addition to building its habitat requirements, you also need to add other terrarium accessories not just for aesthetic purposes but mainly for the purpose of resembling the frog's habitat or environment in the wild. You should also keep in mind some things you should avoid when it comes to creating its terrarium which will be discussed later on in this chapter.

Keep reading to learn the basics about your Pacman frog's habitat requirements. You will be given tips and guidelines on how to create and maintain an ideal habitat for your pet Pacman.

Ideal Habitat for Pacman Frogs

As mentioned earlier in this book, you need to house your pet Pacman in an enclosure or a terrarium because they are quite sensitive creatures that need to be protected from people or other potential threats and mostly because they are the kind of pet that's for observation only.

- **Cage Size**

The rule of thumb when it comes to keeping a Pacman frog is to provide them on a separate enclosure. They shouldn't be mixed with other frogs or even breeds of the same kind because these animals are cannibalistic in nature. They're the kind of frogs that are sit-and-wait predators, so if you place them with other frogs that are smaller breeds, it will be no surprise if they eat them.

Since Pacman frogs are inactive most of the time, they don't need a huge enclosure or terrarium; you can settle with a 10 – gallon tank, this is the minimum. Never go below 10 gallons. You can also reach around 20 gallons but going beyond that is not necessary. The terrarium should also have a screen lid or cage top because some Pacman frog breeds are known to escape.

For tadpoles, you can choose to keep them in a small plastic cage that can be bought at various pet stores. Keep in mind though that it may be difficult to adjust the heat temperature since the casing is plastic, experts recommend buying a glass cage or glass terrariums with a screen lid.

You should also make sure that there are lots of hiding places such as a burrowing land hideout. Also provide branches (for exercise opportunities, although Pacman frogs may not need that) and lots of plants inside. Don't forget to include the water bowl because it will act as a pond for these frogs.

- **Plants, Branches and Bark Bedding**

Pacman frogs love to stay on the ground, and hang around dry litter of leaves pretty much all day, this is how they live in the wild, which is why it's vital that you create the same kind of environment so that they can easily adapt and be comfortable with their new home.

Provide your frog's enclosure with lots of branches and plants or leaves as well as hiding places or areas where they can sit still until you feed them; this will enable them to practice their natural ability, make them feel comfortable in their new home, and will also make them feel close to their natural habitat even in captivity.

Try adding green or brown leaves (preferably a fresh one) because it will make your frog feel safe. Aim to use live plants because it can also help increase as well as maintain humidity inside the enclosure.Keep in mind to only use non – toxic plants to avoid being exposed to chemicals that could adversely affect your frog's health. If you buy a plant from the pet store you may not be sure if it is safe for your frog due to insecticides and toxic fertilizers. Just make sure to properly wash them with soap and water to remove harmful chemical residues.

It's also helpful that you set up bark bedding made out of coconut – fiber at the bottom of the terrarium; your frog might get interested in burrowing it, it is also a good form of exercise.

Create a 5 – 10 cm or 2 – 4 inches of bark bed on the enclosure; just make sure to replace the bedding at least once in a month and constantly remove droppings.

Make sure to clean the small branches if you're going to grab one from outside plants. Also wash the bake branches before using it. You can buy bendy vines at various pet stores - they also make a great cage décor. You may also want to arrange, and re - arrange the branch, vines and plant settings from time to time.

- **Water Bowl**

You should also provide a large but shallow water bowl for your Pacman frog (or a size that is suitable for your petto avoid the risk of drowning) because in the wild these creatures can be found in ponds and freshwater marshes, it will help them cope up with their new environment. You might want to include plants inside the water dish as well. Frogs will need to cool off if the temperature inside is humid, make sure to also place the bowl on the warmer area of the enclosure so that if it gets cold, the water may not be too cold for them. Frequently clean the bowl to maintain cleanliness.

Cage Setup Guidelines

There are many ways on how to set up a great habitat for your Pacman frog, but aside from the materials used for its cage, you also need to include equipment to sustain an adequate living condition for these animals.

Below are some general guidelines you should follow when installing these equipment.

- **Heat Temperature and Lighting**

The temperature inside the enclosure should be measured at 24 – 29 Celsius (75 – 85 F) during the day, and around 18 – 24 Celsius (65 – 75 F) at night. The humidity should be around 50% - 80%, the plants will help regulate humidity so make sure to buy appropriate plants for the enclosure. You can also purchase a hygrometer to measure the moisture of the tank.

The under tank heater or UTH is a better source of heat than incandescent bulbs, although a red bulb can be a supplement during cold days. You should also opt to buy a thermometer to keep track of the temperature inside the cage and be able to adjust the heat or light accordingly.

For the lighting, you can set up a fluorescent fixture or use a UVB light because frogs might prefer subdued lighting. Although most Pacman frogs are nocturnal and do not require direct sunlight, they still need a lighting that mimics night and day, so open the fluorescent lighting for a 12 hours day and night cycle.

- **Substrate and Water Misting**

You need to provide hand spray daily water misting to maintain humidity. The substrate must be moist but not be too wet or soggy.

Cage Maintenance

The enclosure or terrarium should be kept clean at all times, you may want to use a water treatment to make sure that the chlorine, nitrates, ammonia and other harmful materials are not ingested by your frog. Do this at least every week or every other day if you can.

It is also recommended that you frequently clean the water dish of your Pacman frog because they'll be spending most of their time soaked in it, which means that that's where your frog will defacate or urinate.

Thoroughly clean the entire casing to prevent potential illnesses for your frog, and to also keep its environment clean and healthy.

Keep in mind that a great living condition can improve your frog's health and overall lifespan.

Chapter Five: Feeding Your Pacman Frog

Meeting your Pacman frog's nutritional needs is very important to ensure that your pet stays healthy, and strong against diseases. Every kind of frog species have different nutritional requirements, that's why reading this chapter is important because it will focus only on Pacman frog breed. Frogs, like many other pets, should be given the right amount of recommended food for a balanced nutrition because proper diet can also lengthen their life expectancy.

In this section, you'll learn the majority of your pet's nutritional needs; tips on how to feed them as well as recommended foods that are good for their health and foods to avoid.

Nutritional Needs of Pacman Frogs

Pacman frogs in the wild live only at a maximum of 4 years, but in captivity, they live for about about 10 – 15 years in general, the main reason is because of their nutritional diet. The main reason for it obviously, is because these wild caught frogs don't have proper nutrition compared when they are being taken care of. They usually eat fish, huge insects, other frog breeds (sometimes their own kind), worms, as well as small reptiles, amphibians and mammals such as mice. The predator – prey factor in their natural habitats is also a major cause of their short lifespan.

Basic Feeding Ingredients

Pacman frogs are primarily insectivores and carnivores, they usually feed on different kinds of worms such as mealworms, waxworms, earthworms, live or canned silkworms as well as small creatures like crickets, cockroaches, snails, caterpillars, and grasshoppers. They are also known to eat mice, rodents and feeder fish. The more varied, the better because it will provide your pet with a balanced nutrition.

All prey items should be dusted or gut – loaded with calcium supplements and vitamin D3 especially for tadpoles or young Pacman frogs to assist them in bone growth. You need to also give them a multi – vitamin at least once a week.

You can occasionally feed them with a pre – killed rodents or mice, however, experts and vets don't recommend it because these animals are high in fat and low in calcium, aside from that, if you feed your frog with a rodent or a rat, most of the time it results in obesity, deficiencies, and shorten lifespan.

Feeding Amount for Pacman Frogs:

Pacman frogs should be fed every 2 to 3 days during the evening (since they are awake at night), if the insects or the gut – loaded food is not fully consumed on the night you feed them, you can just lessen the amount the following night until they will be able to consume it.

For baby frogs or tadpoles, they need a gut – loaded diet to aid in its growth and also strengthen their body against illnesses.

In the next sections, you'll be given information on how to properly gut – load your Pacman frog's food.

Gut - load

Gut loading of food is a kind of process where you increase the nutritional value of the insects that you feed to your Pacman frog. The concept is very simple, since we all live in an ecosystem, we all benefit from one another in various ways. A great example is the eagle, eagles eat snakes, while snakes eat rodents or chickens, chickens feed on worms, and worms feed in various sources. It is same with Pacman frogs in the wild, their insect preys also feed on many different nutrition sources within that ecosystem, which makes balance nutrition. However, in captivity, it's just impossible to create that kind of natural cycle, so in order to replicate that you as the owner should properly gut load the food that you feed your frog.

You need to also properly feed the insects or the prey a special diet or good nutrition so that in the end your Pacman frog will benefit from that very balanced and proper nutrition.

In order for you to gut load the food of your Pacman frog you should supplement it with a multivitamin powder with calcium. The calcium should be higher than phosphorus, because high phosphorus inhibits calcium absorption. The supplements should also be low in oxalates.

Unfortunately, most commercial gut loads are low in calcium which may not be sufficient for your frog's nutritional needs. The great thing is that you can actually create a Do – It – Yourself gut load that contains the needed nutrients for your pet at home. It's very easy to make and quite inexpensive.

Here are the following tips on how to create your own gut load:

- Get at least two or three options (either fruits or vegetables) from the store in which you can use as gut load to your frog's food, and then just rotate them every now and then.

- Always wash all the produce to rinse off any pesticide or chemical residues; peel the fruit's skin cover or cut the veggies because sometimes the pesticide or chemical components stick to the fruit or vegetable.

- The nutrients will be passed on to your frog around 2 – 3 weeks after you feed them.

Primary Gut – loading Ingredients

The following suggested ingredients should be the primary component of your gut load. They are high in calcium, low in oxalates, phosphorus, and goitrogens.

- Mustard greens
- Dandelion leaves
- Turnip Greens
- Collard Greens
- Papaya
- Escarole Lettuce
- Watercress
- Alfalfa

Secondary Gut – loading Ingredients

The following suggested ingredients are only secondary components for your gut load. They are only moderately high in calcium, has a relatively low oxalates, phosphorus, and goitrogens components. They are additional ingredients for your gut – load.

- Sweet Potato

- Carrots
- Butternut
- Mango
- Orange
- Kale
- Apples
- Squash
- Beet Greens
- Bok Choy
- Blackberries
- Green beans

Dry Gut – loading Ingredients:

The primary and secondary ingredients can also be mixed with dry gut load and homemade mixes for a well – rounded nutrition.

- Sunflower seeds (organic and non – salted)
- Bee pollen
- Dried Seaweed
- Spirulina
- Flax seed
- Almonds (organic and non – salted)

Toxic Gut – Loading Ingredients

The following suggested ingredients should be avoided and must not be included in your gut – load. They are very low in calcium.

- Cabbage
- Potatoes
- Iceberg Lettuce
- Romain Lettuce
- Spinach
- Broccoli
- Tomatoes
- Grains
- Corns
- Oats
- Beans
- Meat
- Eggs
- Cereals
- Cat food/ Dog food
- Fish food
- Canned/ dead insects

Important Reminder

If you feed your frog with meat or a carnivore diet, it can potentially be fatal because these creatures can suffocate or choke your Pacman frog to death because it might be larger than their digestive system. Only feed your frog an all – insect diet plus good gut loaded ingredients and supplementation.

Supplementation

Calcium is very important to your Pacman frog diet as well as vitamins that can be found in powdered supplements. You should sprinkle a small amount of these powdered supplements in the feeder insect before giving them to your Pacman frog.

Feeding Tips

Below are some feeding tips you can easily follow and implement when feeding your Pacman frog:

- Make sure to follow the feeding amount guidelines at the beginning of this chapter.

- If you are going to hand – feed your frogs with meat make sure to get your hand or fingers out of the way because they might mistake it as a food, although, if you frequently hand – fed them they'll eventually recognize that it is a non – food entity.

- If you are feeding crickets or similar insects to your Pacman frog, you should first gut loaded it with calcium enriched vegetables few hours before feeding them to your frog.

- Keep in mind that inadequate dietary calcium may lead to various illnesses.

Chapter Six: The Life Cycle of a Pacman Frog

Knowing the life cycle of frogs is not only educational but also quite interesting because their life cycle stage is very similar to butterflies. They starts out as something small, then evolves into a disgusting, and often times gross kind of creatures during their tadpole stage, but eventually they turn into this colorful and exotic species that we are all fond off, sometimes with proper nutrients and a broken spell from a wicked witch can also turn them into a prince! Okay, maybe not.

As with the traditional definition of amphibians, frogs can live in both land and water. But to be more precise about it, frogs as amphibians are unique in their evolution;

they all begin their journey from being a tiny egg to a creature that lives in water, and eventually metamorphose to tadpoles with gills before turning into colorful adult breeds. The permeable skin of amphibians also functions as secondary respiratory surfaces. Frogs comprise about 90% of the amphibian world.

Reproduction

If you want to stimulate your Pacman frogs to breed, they usually will need 2 months of cooling period beforehand. You should also start reducing the humidity level and heat temperature (by about 70 degrees Fahrenheit) of the enclosure to encourage your pet to go into estivation. Once they are undergoing this process, do not attempt to feed them or dig them up on the ground.

After being done with estivation, your frog needs to experience a "rainy season," you can do this through putting your Pacman frog in a rain chamber or you could also try misting the terrarium more frequently. You should stop doing this once your frogs have bred. Start providing your pets with plants so that the female frog can attach their eggs in it. Pacman frogs lay around 1,000 – 2,000 eggs. Once your female frog laid them, separate it immediately because it is an animal instinct to eat the eggs or their offspring.

In about 2 – 4 days you can expect the eggs to hatch, by that time you should place additional water inside the enclosure.

The Eggs or Frogspawn

The choice of location for egg laying is to enable the small tadpoles to fall directly into water after they hatch. The eggs of a Pacman frog are white and small, and start out encased in a jelly-like substance which protects them until they hatch some 2 - 4 days later. When the eggs hatch, the tadpoles that emerge fall directly into the water below, where they begin swimming using their tail. These larvae are initially adapted solely to an aquatic lifestyle.

When several eggs are clumped together, this is known collectively as frogspawn. Interestingly, larvae are able to detect vibrations caused by nearby predators, and as a matter of protection – and to avoid being eaten – the eggs will actually hatch earlier than usual. This is known as phenotypic plasticity, where eggs or embryos hatch early as a manner of self-protection.

Larvae or Tadpoles

The tiny brown tadpole looks a lot like a fish because they breathe using gills and they use their tails for swimming. This part or phase of their life usually lasts from 7 - 9 weeks.

As the tadpoles grow, they begin to develop legs which enable them to crawl out of the water and towards land. What takes place next is known as apoptosis, a kind of controlled cell death which results in the reabsorption of the organs that have become redundant. Thus, the frog's tail begins to shrink until it has been fully absorbed. Eventually, the lungs develop and the gills and gill pouch eventually disappear because it was being replaced by their legs, as they metamorphose into young frogs, which they must do before the pools dry out. As metamorphosis continues, eyes are repositioned and eyelids are formed.

The legs, their jaws, and their tongue eventually form as well. The skin also becomes thicker and tougher. When the tail is gone, the tiny new frog can begin to live its life out of the water, moving into hiding places in the plants near the pool until it can eventually use its feet and the powerful suction cups on their toes to leap and move around.

Froglets or Young Frogs

The Pacman frog's appearance and skin coloring are somewhat darkish brown in color when they were young or during their tadpole stage, but when they become adult frogs they eventually turn into their present vivid colors that is mostly green and yellow. Their eyes are usually black in color during their tadpole years.

Adult Frogs

The adult Pacman frog has large and bulging brightly colored red or black eyes. The sides are striped with green and yellow colors. Their mouths and legs are usually the same color as their body markings and patterns.

Adult females are usually about 6 - 7 inches or 15 cm while males only measure about 2 - 4 inches or 10 cm (still depends on the breed). The measurements both pertain to its length and wideness because Pacman frogs' body structure is equally wide and long. They usually reached maturity around 1 – 2 years.

Chapter Seven: Caring Guidelines for Pacman Frogs

The chapter about Pacman frogs' requirements has already given you an idea on how to build a cage, the materials needed for an enclosure, as well as the equipment that needs to be installed; you have also learned general information about the Pacman frog breed, and also an introduction of their characteristics.

In this chapter you will be given further information about their behaviors and how to handle them, as well as give you some tips on how to take care of them so that they can be happy in their new home.

Temperament of Pacman Frogs

The different breeds of Pacman frogs are great pets especially for first – time frog or amphibian owners mainly because they are low maintenance and relatively easy to keep. However, there is one major red flag that you need to be aware of about your Pacman frogs – they are predators. Unlike most frogs in the wild, Pacman frogs are "silent killers," and instead of being the prey as most frogs are, these species in general are a solid predator. That's why it's important that you don't mix them with smaller frog species, other amphibian breeds, or even another Pacman frog because they'll end up killing one another.

They can be quite aggressive especially when you feed them or sometimes when you handle them. As previously mentioned, frogs in general don't like to be handled too often because they're very sensitive and it could be a source of stress for your pet if they're always being touched – it could also adversely affect your pet's health. The skin of amphibians in general is absorbent and it is very oily; the skin of people has salt which is why it could somehow cause them harm. If you really need to constantly hold them or if holding them is unavoidable, it's recommended that you washed your hands beforehand and also use latex gloves.

Pacman frogs might mistake you as a threat or might accidentally eat your finger whenever you are hand feeding them, keep in mind that they're the only frog breed that has teeth and is also known for its powerful jaw which could grip any predator – or finger for that matter. If you got bitten by your pet, it's going to be a painful experience; you might need to apply an antiseptic or better yet go to a clinic or nearby hospital to clean up that wound.

It's crucial that if in any case your finger got caught up in your frog's jaw, you shouldn't try to pull your hand because you can potentially damage your Pacman's jaw, try to hold the frog under a faucet or running water to encourage him or her to let go of your hand or finger.

Frog Sloughing

Horned frogs or Pacman frogs regularly shed their skin as they grow and mature. The old skin of your frog will be pushed off using their hind legs, until it is peeled off to their backend. Once the skin is completely shed off completely, your frog will normally eat it. The peeled off skin is pushed towards the mouth using their legs.

This actually sounds disgusting but this kind of behavior is normal among frogs.

Frog Estivation

Estivation is the hibernation period that is very common among Pacman frogs, this usually happens during cold months.

The process involves the frog creating a cocoon or shell using its old skin to seal them off in moisture. Once this process is done, the frogs then buries itself underground and waits until the summer.

You don't have to worry about your Pacman frog completely burying themselves on the ground and disappearing for a long time if your temperatures inside the enclosure are regulated and controlled. However, if your temperature drops or if the enclosure especially during cold months isn't providing them enough heat, then your frog might start to estivate.

If your Pacman frog estivates, you shouldn't disturb or attempt to feed him or her, instead try using fresh water (preferably de-chlorinated) and gradually raise the heat temperature or make it more humid inside the terrarium. This could help awaken your Pacman frog, make them come out of their shell and bring them back to doing normal behavior.

Pacman Frog Grooming

Unlike other household pets, you cannot and shouldn't attempt to give your frog a bath or thoroughly clean them; you could potentially kill them if you apply any kind of bathing products! However, it's still important that you maintain their hygiene to avoid any diseases that could harm your Pacman frog through cleaning their terrarium or enclosure.

You can use cleaning accessories such as brush to remove dirt inside the terrarium, but make sure that before you do this, you should transfer first your Pacman frog to another enclosure. Don't attempt to clean it while your pet is inside. You can also try to use a soft net or a small mesh to keep your frog away and protected while you do habitat maintenance. Be extra cautious on the kind of cleaning supplies you will use to clean the dirt, make sure that it is non – toxic or only contains a low amount of chemical. Also make sure to rinse the cage thoroughly to avoid any chemical or soap residue.

You should also keep in mind that amphibians secrete toxins, be careful about these frog secretions and don't let it get to your eyes, mouth or any open wounds. It can be harmful to your health.

Chapter Eight: Breeding Your Pacman Frog

If keeping a Pacman frog is already challenging enough for you especially for first time owners, you might just want to stick to becoming an expert at it for a while before deciding to breed more of them. This chapter may not be suitable for everyone, even if you are already a frog owner. Handling and breeding female Pacman frogs can be quite challenging and it can take much of your time. Breeding can be difficult because these creatures are delicate and very sensitive, however if you think you're up for the challenge, or would just want to know how breeding works, the information in this chapter can be useful for you. Happy breeding!

Sexing

Before you breed your frog to another Pacman breed, you should first determine their gender and the only way you can do that is through listening. Male frogs call or make a particular sound if they wanted to mate or during their mating season. Male frogs' appearance usually exhibits a darker color on their throats, and they also tend to develop a nuptial pad. Another way to identify their sex is through observing a female and male frog; females are usually larger and more rounded in shape than male Pacman frogs.

Breeding Basics

If you want to stimulate your Pacman frogs to breed, they usually will need 2 months of cooling period beforehand. Consider it as preparation for your frogs before they engage into breeding. You can help in their cooling period if by providing a deep sphagnum moss and water bowl because they'll probably opt to stay there; you should also start reducing the humidity level and heat temperature (by about 70 degrees Fahrenheit) of the enclosure to encourage your pet to go into estivation. Once they are undergoing this process, do not attempt to feed them or dig them up on the ground.

After being done with estivation, your frog needs to experience a "rainy season," you can do this through putting your Pacman frog in a rain chamber or you could also try misting the terrarium more frequently. You should stop doing this once your frogs have bred. Start providing your pets with plants so that the female frog can attach their eggs in it.

Spawning

Spawning is another term for hatching for frog species. Pacman frogs lay around 1,000 – 2,000 eggs! Once your female frog laid them, separate it immediately because it is an animal instinct to eat the eggs or their offspring. In about 2 – 4 days you can expect the eggs to hatch, by that time you should place additional water inside the enclosure.

Tadpole Maintenance

Once the eggs hatched, they are now called tadpoles. Tadpole management can take lots of your time so make sure to think about it twice or thrice before deciding to breed your frogs.

Tadpoles are cannibals in general; they will eat each other if you put them all in one enclosure. So to solve this problem, you should place the tadpoles in a small jar or in a separate enclosure. However, you have to make sure that you always clean the separate jars which could take a lot of work (imagine providing or cleaning 1,000+ jars? Okay maybe that's exaggeration, but you get the point).

You can also try to place them all in a large terrarium filled with plants (live plants are preferred). If you do this you can lose a couple of tadpoles due to cannibalism but it's much more convenient. You just have to sprinkle their food (a tubifex or chopped earthworms) on the floor of the terrarium so that the tadpoles will just swim down, eat their food and then hide within the plants. You need to also clean and replace the water inside the tanks but its advantage is that you just need to clean one tank as compared to various jars.

Tadpole Metamorphosis

After one month, the tadpoles will begin to transform into juvenile frogs, by this point they will need to be placed out of water, which means that it's another husbandry setup. You have to make sure that you separate them individually if you want to keep these frogs not ending up in each other's mouth. You can place them in their own plastic cup if you want to feed them. Tadpoles grow rapidly and will eat anything you feed them such as mealworms, goldfish and even other frogs.

Pacman frogs and tadpoles in general are fun to breed, their metamorphosis is very interesting to watch as time goes by, but you need to really invest a huge amount of your time if you want to keep them until they reached adulthood.

Tips for Breeding Pacman Frogs

- The reason why most breeders recommend a higher ratio of frogs than a simple breeding pair is because competition seems to encourage breeding. More males than females can lead the males to be more energetic in their reproductive behavior, thus increasing the odds of a successful breeding.

- Frogs are said to be sensitive to barometric pressure, so even when you are artificially creating rainy conditions within their enclosure, you might want to wait until it an actual storm front before moving your frogs into the rain chamber as this has been said to increase the chances of successful mating.

- Throughout the preparation for breeding and the breeding process itself, up to the laying of the eggs and the hatching of the eggs, part of the water in the container should always be changed daily. This prevents the accumulation of waste in the water that may eventually cause illness or disease in the frogs or the eggs and tadpoles.

- Sometimes, the female will also lay eggs on the side of the rain chamber. This is okay as long as the eggs are still located above water. While some breeders remove the leaves and move the eggs to a different container, others simply remove the adults and leave the eggs in the rain chamber. The important thing is to separate the adults from the eggs after they have been laid. This is to prevent the adults from feeding on or climbing on the leaves, damaging, or dislodging the eggs. Should the eggs be knocked into the water, these will certainly drown.

- Should the female eggs successively on different nights, you might want to cut each leaf off and remove them to a different container after the eggs are laid. Just make sure to position the leaves and the eggs securely over water.

The metamorphosed tadpoles are quite capable of scaling the sides of the aquarium using their new legs, so make sure that the top is secured with a screen top. You might also want to provide them with a place to climb onto after their legs have developed. Floating driftwood or cork bark often works well.

Chapter Nine: Keeping Your Pacman Frog Healthy

Once you've bought a healthy Pacman frog, you must know how to keep it healthy. What do they need? How much should you feed them? What are the symptoms of possible diseases? You should be able to tell when your Pacman frog needs a trip to the vet.

In this chapter, you will be given information about the potential illnesses that could threaten your frog's health. Having an idea and information about these diseases can make you be aware of its potential threats and be able to prevent it before it affects your pet frog.

Common Health Problems

Pacman frogs can be affected by a number of different health problems and they are generally not specific to any particular breed. Feeding your Pacman frog a nutritious diet will go a long way in securing his total health and well - being, but sometimes frogs get ill anyway. If you want to make sure that your pet gets the treatment he needs as quickly as possible you need to learn how to identify the symptoms of disease. These symptoms are not always obvious either; your Pacman frog may not show any outward or noticeable signs because they are not an active breed. That's why it's also important that you check on your frog every now and then and take the time to observe its physical appearance or catch any sign of unusual behavior.

The more time you spend with your pet frog, the more you will come to understand its behavior – this is the key to catching health problems early. At the first sign that something is wrong with your pet you should take inventory of his symptoms – both physical and behavioral – so you can relay them to your veterinarian who will then make a diagnosis and prescribe a course of treatment. The sooner you identify these symptoms, the sooner your vet can take action and the more likely your Pacman frog will be able to make a full recovery. Generally, though frogs are healthy but since they are captive – bred, the stresses of the environment or husbandry are the causes of its illnesses.

Pacman frog can be prone to a wide variety of diseases or infections, though some are more common than others. For the benefit your Pacman frog's long-term health, take the time to learn the causes, symptoms, and treatment options for some of the most common health problems. Besides red flags, it is best to be in the know when it comes to what these red flags mean. Pacman frogs have some common health issues you can find by identifying the symptoms or causes.

Here are some of the common health issues to look out for:

Common Conditions Affecting Pacman Frogs

Some of the common conditions that affect Pacman frogs include the following:

- Metabolic Bone Disease
- Toxic Out Syndrome
- Water Edema Syndrome
- Bacterial Infections
- Fungal Infection
- Endoparasites
- Blindness
- Impaction
- Obesity

Metabolic Bone Disease

This illness is not just common among frogs but also to amphibians (and even reptiles) in general. This disease is caused by a lack in dietary calcium, improper lighting, and also imbalanced nutrition.

As mentioned earlier in the feeding chapter of the book, your frog should have the right amount of calcium and you should sprinkle its food with enough Vitamin D3. If the calcium levels are low, the body will be forced to get calcium source straight from the bones so that there will be enough energy for the body to function especially for muscle movements and metabolism. The effect however is that the bones becomes weak and eventually brittle, which could cause bone deformities in your pet frog.

The usual signs you should look out for is droopy lower jaw, failure to grab prey, muscle twitching, listlessness, and backbone and pelvic deformities.

If your frog gets affected with this disorder it cannot be reversed but the good news is that the process of progression of the disease can be stopped. You can immediately treat it by coating or gut – loading its food with calcium and Vitamin D3. If you have seen your frog having problems grabbing or keeping its prey intact in their jaws because it's too soft chances are that your pet is being affected with MBD, make sure to administer the calcium plus the Vit. D3 using a syringe directly on its mouth at least every 1 – 2 days until you sees the bones harden up.

If prevented, the bones can be treated with proper medications, and it can heal over time. Proper husbandry such as enough access to UVB lighting as well as proper nutrition can correct the calcium imbalance in the body.

Toxic Out Syndrome

Toxic Out Syndrome is usually caused by dirty water, the reason for this is because a frog's skin absorbs water either from the substrate or the water bowl/dish, that's why if you do not frequently replace or replenish the water, it's going to become contaminated with bacteria and other toxic wastes that the frog itself secrete which could be absorbed by your pet and can lead to this syndrome.

The usual symptoms of toxic out syndrome include erratic jumping and spastic extensions of the hind limbs, listlessness, and cloudy eyes.

Fortunately this syndrome is easily treatable, you just need to place your frog in its water bowl with clean water, and just leave them there for about 4 hours, after which you need to replace the water until you notice that the signs of the syndrome are fading away. If you want to prevent this from happening in the future, you should always clean the terrarium and make it a habit to replenish the water that was used for the day so that your frog won't be able to absorb contaminated water in their skin because it could also result to other illnesses.

Water Edema Syndrome

The major sign of Water Edema syndrome is when your frog starts to swell up or appears like a squishy water bag. The main reason behind this is that the water is being retained on their bodies because their kidneys or heart are damaged or has some issues. Until now, there's no information on how to prevent this from happening, the best thing you can do is to limit the water available or immediately bring your pet to the vet so that they can do proper procedures.

Usually the vets will recommend doing a small incisions to release the water, however it may not always be work out, and they could likely absorb unwanted water again once they are back on their enclosures.

Bacterial Infections

Like any other creatures, even humans for that matter are constantly exposed to bacterial infections. Thankfully, each of us – humans or animals have built – in immune system that fights the virus or bacteria that penetrate the body and protect it from further illnesses. However, in the case of frogs, if your pet frog is stressed because of the environment or otherwise, its immune system can become weak which means that the bacteria can invade easily.

The main causes of bacterial infections are contaminated water, unregulated temperatures inside the closure or inappropriate handling and feeding, so to be able to prevent this, proper husbandry is the answer. You can reduce the stress by always making sure that you keep in mind your frog's hygiene.

The most common signs include loss of appetite, listlessness, cloudy eyes, redness on the underside of the belly and the thighs, and excessive skin sloughing with shed skin released in the water. Although symptoms vary, you should be able to spot one of these symptoms in your Pacman frog. Extreme neurological or behavioral signs can also be noticed if the infection is not immediately prevented.

Red leg is the most common bacterial infection that could lead to rapid illness and could also be fatal. Make sure to bring your pet to the doctor so that your vet can prescribe the proper medications and treatment. Usually vets prescribe antibiotics to treat bacterial infections.

Fungal Infection

Fungal infections are usually common among tadpoles or juvenile Pacman frogs. It can infect wounds or the skin of your pet. You can easily treat it by removing your frog from the water, and use hydrogen peroxide, or malachite green. Just apply it to the infected area using a cotton ball.

Endoparasites

Endoparasites in frogs include having roundworms, tapeworms and pinworms inside the intestines. A healthy dose of endoparasites actually help in the digestion of food, but too much can of course harm your frog. There aren't any physical signs that your Pacman frog contain too much intestinal parasites, so it's highly recommended that you bring your frog to the vet every now and then for a check-up, and so that your vet can treat it as soon as possible.

Usually the most common cause of Endoparasite is by placing frogs in one enclosure because parasites are transferrable. This is also the reason why you need to quarantine your pet first.

Blindness

Blindness among frogs is caused by frequently feeding mice or rodents; these creatures are high in fat which is why it could cause the build-up of lipids in the corneas or eyes of the frog. As much as possible avoid feeding your Pacman frog and make sure that its diet is a low-fat one.

Impaction

Impaction among frogs is often caused by the ingestion of substrate when they are trying to grab their prey or when they ingested chunks of gravel found in the floor of the terrarium. These chunks could potentially block the intestinal tract of the frog.

In order for you to prevent this from happening you should house your Pacman frog in alternate substrate like a moist coir, moss or foam rubber that has a huge water container.

One way for you to know if your frog is suffering from impaction is if you notice its belly bulging, or if you feel a hard lump around it. Usually the frog will excrete the substrate it ingested after a few weeks, but if such condition persist, contact your vet immediately and have it removed.

Obesity

Pacman frogs are large in size compare to other frog species, and they are cannibals in general but it doesn't mean that they also require huge amount of food; you as the owner should still regulate their food intake to maintain a normal and healthy weight.

Some owners increase their frog's size through feeding the adult or mature frog's a similar feeding schedule of a juvenile or young frogs (which is frequent than normal because they need more food for their growth) however, it's obviously inappropriate once your Pacman frog reached its full size. Others try to feed their frogs with a prey that is larger than their pet's size which could also pose a threat to its overall health.

Pacman frogs reach its full adult size in 2 – 3 years; once they reached their full – size most of the food they consume will be converted to fat and not so much use for the muscle or bone building because they're already passed that stage. As a result, the frog will become obese, which could also lead to a shortened lifespan.

For you to prevent obesity follow this feeding schedule for your frog:

- Froglets (2 inches): Feed supplemented 3 - week gut - loaded crickets every 1 - 2 days

- Juvenile Frogs: Feed supplemented 3 - week old crickets; pre-killed mice and gut - loaded worms every 2 - 3 days.

- Adult frogs: Feed supplemented gut - loaded crickets or worms, roaches or other night crawlers every 7-10 days.

Pacman Frog Care Sheet

Congratulate yourself! You are now on your way to becoming a very well-informed and pro-active Pacman frog owner! Finishing this book is a huge milestone for you and your future or present pet frog but before this ultimate guide comes to an end, keep in mind the most important things you have acquired through reading this book. In the previous chapters, we have discussed the characteristics of a Pacman frog – its requirements, the costs of keeping it as a pet, how to keep it healthy, and proper breeding practices. It may be a lot of information to take in, so we have compiled a care sheet to summarize the information you can find in this book.

1.) Basic Pacman Frog Information

Scientific Name: Agalychnis callidryas

Kingdom: Animalia

Phylum: Chordata

Class: Amphibia

Order: Anura

Family: Ceratophryidae

Genus: Ceratophrys

Regions of Origin: Argentina, Brazil, Ecuador, Peru, Uruguay, Paraguay

Primary Habitat: Dry subtropical and tropical forests, dry savannahs, freshwater marshes, shrub lands

Adult Male Size: 2 - 4 inches or 10 cm

Adult Female Size: 6 - 7 inches or 15 cm

Feeds On: Mice, Rats, Lizards, Rodents

Description: They are generally large and have a very wide mouth.

Colors and Markings: Comes in various colors that are all unique because of its special combination of markings. The most common colors for Pacman frogs are red, yellow, green, and dark brown with spots or bright markings on their skin.

Primary Behavioral Characteristics: terrestrial, lazy and carnivorous

Health Conditions: Metabolic Bone Disease, Bacterial infection, Toxic Out Syndrome, Fungal Infection, Blindness, Obesity, Impaction, Endoparasites and Water Edema Syndrome.

Lifespan: average of 15 years, but may live longer

2.) Habitat Requirements

Recommended Equipment: standard 10 - 20 gallon tank or terrarium secured with a screen top, and equipped with substrate, water dish, and climbing and hiding structures such as branches, artificial or natural plants with broad leaves, bark bedding

Recommended Temperature: 24 – 29 Celsius (75 – 85 F) during the day, and around 18 – 24 Celsius (65 – 75 F) at night

Recommended Humidity Level: 50% - 80%,

Cleaning Frequency: Spot cleaning daily, with a more thorough cleaning at least once a week

3.) Feeding and Diet

Primary Diet: Crickets, moths, flies and other insects, and sometimes a variety of worms

Feeding Frequency (tadpoles): Feed 2-3 times a week

Feeding Frequency (juvenile): Feed daily or up to 4 times a week

Feeding Frequency (adult): Every 2-3 days

Water: Clean water in a water dish should always be freely available

4.) Breeding Information

Age of Sexual Maturity: Sexual maturity is reached at around 1 - 2 years

Estivation Temperature: 70 degrees Fahrenheit

Clutch Size: 1,000 – 2,000 eggs

Incubation: 2 – 4 days

Website Resources for Your Pacman Frogs

Here are some website resources for your Pacman housing and feeding needs, we also included websites for cage accessories or décor and cleaning supplies for your terrariums.

Habitat Enclosure

Petmountain.com
<http://www.petmountain.com/category/811/1/frog-habitats.html>

Amazon.com
<https://www.amazon.com/Exo-Terra-PT2602-Rainforest-Habitat/dp/B001B5DIMK>

Stuccu.com
<http://n.stuccu.com/s/Frog+Cages>

Amazing Amazon
<https://www.amazingamazon.com.au/frog-cages-enclosures.html>

Vivarium For Sale
<http://vivariumforsale.com/>

Preloved UK
<http://www.preloved.co.uk/classifieds/for-sale/uk/frog+tank>

Glass Box Tropicals
<https://www.glassboxtropicals.com/>

Black Jungle Terrariums Supply
<http://www.blackjungleterrariumsupply.com/>

Gumtree
<https://www.gumtree.com/pet-equipment-accessories/uk/vivarium>

Twig Terrariums

<http://twigterrariums.com/collections/readymade-terrariums>

Frog Food

Petmountain.com
<http://www.petmountain.com/category/297/1/frog-newt-food.html>

Josh's Frogs – Live Insects
<https://www.joshsfrogs.com/live-insects-feeders.html>

Josh's Frogs – Dry Pellets
https://www.joshsfrogs.com/dry-pelleted-food.html

Amazing Amazon
<https://www.amazingamazon.com.au/reptiles-melbourne-victoria-australia-for-sale/frogs-for-sale-victoria/food-for-frogs.html>

Pisces Pros
<http://www.piscespros.com/frog-food/>

Petco
<http://www.petco.com/shop/en/petcostore/category/reptile/live-reptiles/frogs-and-toads>

Frogs.Org
<https://frogs.org.au/live-foods/>

Stuccu.com
<http://n.stuccu.com/s/Frog+Food>

Fine Comb
<http://finecomb.com>

Cage Accessories

Josh's Frogs - Pacman Frog Kits
<https://www.joshsfrogs.com/complete-care-kits/frog-kits/pacman-frog-kits.html>

Etsy
<https://www.etsy.com/market/terrarium_kit>

Gardners.com
<http://www.gardeners.com/buy/diy-terrarium-kit/8590327.html>

Air Plant Supply
<https://www.airplantsupplyco.com/collections/premium-terrariums>

Twig Terrariums

<http://twigterrariums.com/collections/diy-kits>

Shop Terrain
<http://www.shopterrain.com/terrariums/>

Juicy Kits
<https://www.juicykits.com/>

Petmountain.com – Frog Decor
<http://www.petmountain.com/category/809/1/frog-decor.html>

Petmountain.com – Frog Food Bowls
<http://www.petmountain.com/category/810/1/frog-food-bowls.html>

Black Jungle Terrariums Supply
<http://www.blackjungleterrariumsupply.com/Plants_c_1.html>

Terrarium Cleaning Supplies

Petsmart
<http://www.petsmart.com/reptile/supplies/cleaning-and-odor-removers/>

Reptile Direct
<http://www.reptiledirect.com/cleaners.aspx>

Big Al's Pets
<https://www.bigalspets.com/reptiles/cleaning-supplies.html>

Pet Discounters
<http://www.petdiscounters.com/Reptile-Terrarium-Cleaning-Supplies_c_2482.html>

Nature Box Pet Emporium
<http://www.natureboxpetemporium.com/cleaning-supplies/>

All Reptiles Canada
<https://allreptiles.ca/supplies/cleaning/rzilla-terrarium-cleaner.html>

The Tye Dyed Iguana
<http://thetyedyediguana.com/terrarium-cleaner/>

Canadian Pet Connection
<https://www.canadianpetconnection.com/collections/reptile-cleaning-supplies/products/zilla-limescale-remover-terrarium-cleaner>

Index

L

M

N

O

P

R

Photo Credits

Page 1 Photo by user Mike Baird via Wikimedia Commons,

https://commons.wikimedia.org/wiki/File:Pacman_Frog,_Ar
gentine_Wide-mouth_Frog,_Ceratophrys_ornata.jpg

Page 8 Photo by user Grosscha via Wikimedia Commons,

https://commons.wikimedia.org/wiki/File:Ceratophrys_orna
ta_(Pacman_Frog).JPG

Page 19 Photo by user Chris Vaughan via Flickr.com,

https://www.flickr.com/photos/grumpychris/57735652/

Page 34 Photo by user Deana Hunter via Flickr.com,

https://www.flickr.com/photos/hunter5/487060138/

Page 46 Photo by user persianpunisher via Flickr.com,

https://www.flickr.com/photos/81484542@N00/2480932779/

Page 54 Photo by user persianpunisher via Flickr.com, https://www.flickr.com/photos/81484542@N00/2445330755/

Page 65 Photo by user Gianmaria M. via Flickr.com, https://www.flickr.com/photos/37895381@N05/3509307330/

Page Photo by user WedlockPictures via Flickr.com, https://www.flickr.com/photos/wedlockpictures/1185808798 5/

Page 71 Photo by user Kate Schreiber via Flickr.com, https://www.flickr.com/photos/115521320@N03/12149384286 /

Page 76 Photo by user David Karp via Flickr.com, https://www.flickr.com/photos/dave_the_drain/28547105065 /in/photolist

Page 83 Photo by user Brian Gratwicke via Flickr.com, https://www.flickr.com/photos/briangratwicke/1952018479/i n/photolist

References

A Set-up Guide for Your New Pacman Frog – Petsmart.com

http://www.petsmart.com/learning-center/reptile-care/a-set-up-guide-for-your-new-pacman-frog/A0198.html

Ceratophrys – Wikipedia.org

https://en.wikipedia.org/wiki/Ceratophrys

Horned Frog

http://amphibiancare.com/2005/06/05/horned-frogs/

Horned Frog Care – The Amphibian UK

http://www.theamphibian.co.uk/horned_frog_care_sheet.htm

Ornate Horn Frog (Pacman Frog) – LLL Reptile

https://www.lllreptile.com/articles/4-ornate-horn-frog-pacman-frog/

Pacman Care Sheet – Reptiles Magazine

http://www.reptilesmagazine.com/Care-Sheets/Pac-Man-Frog/

Pacman Frogs as Pets – The Spruce

https://www.thespruce.com/pacman-frogs-as-pets-1236716

Pacman – Petco.com

https://www.petco.com/content/petco/PetcoStore/en_US/pet-services/resource-center/caresheets/pac-man-frog.html

Pac Man Frog – Frog World

http://frogworld.net/pac-man-frog/

Pacman Frog Care Sheet – Exotic Pets Resources

http://www.exoticpetsresources.com/amphibians/frogs/pacman-frog/pacman-frog-care-sheet/

Pacman Frog Factoids – Aqua Land Pets Plus

http://aqualandpetsplus.com/Frog,%20Pac%20Man.htm

Feeding Baby
Cynthia Cherry
978-1941070000

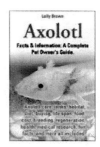

Axolotl
Lolly Brown
978-0989658430

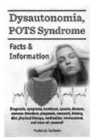

Dysautonomia, POTS
Syndrome
Frederick Earlstein
978-0989658485

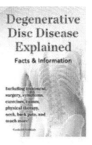

Degenerative Disc
Disease Explained
Frederick Earlstein
978-0989658485

Sinusitis, Hay Fever,
Allergic Rhinitis Explained
Frederick Earlstein
978-1941070024

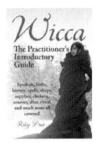

Wicca
Riley Star
978-1941070130

Zombie Apocalypse
Rex Cutty
978-1941070154

Capybara
Lolly Brown
978-1941070062

Eels As Pets
Lolly Brown
978-1941070167

Scabies and Lice Explained
Frederick Earlstein
978-1941070017

Saltwater Fish As Pets
Lolly Brown
978-0989658461

Torticollis Explained
Frederick Earlstein
978-1941070055

Kennel Cough
Lolly Brown
978-0989658409

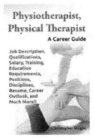

Physiotherapist, Physical
Therapist
Christopher Wright
978-0989658492

Rats, Mice, and Dormice
As Pets
Lolly Brown
978-1941070079

Wallaby and Wallaroo Care
Lolly Brown
978-1941070031

Bodybuilding Supplements
Explained
Jon Shelton
978-1941070239

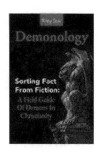

Demonology
Riley Star
978-19401070314

Pigeon Racing
Lolly Brown
978-1941070307

Dwarf Hamster
Lolly Brown
978-1941070390

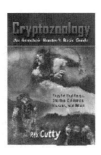

Cryptozoology
Rex Cutty
978-1941070406

Eye Strain
Frederick Earlstein
978-1941070369

Inez The Miniature Elephant
Asher Ray
978-1941070353

Vampire Apocalypse
Rex Cutty
978-1941070321

Made in the USA
Columbia, SC
23 October 2018